D

UNIFORMS

UNIFORMS

BILL DUNN

LAURENCE KING PUBLISHING

CONTENTS

INTRODUCTION

The modern world seems to have fallen out of love with the uniform. The days of the redoubtable English 'city gent' commuter striding across London Bridge sporting the regulatory bowler hat, pinstripes and tightly furled umbrella are gone; schoolboys rarely wear caps, and even policemen seem to be dressing down in trendy combats and sweaters. But look carefully and uniforms are still with us, they've just moved with the times. The student serving you coffee from a global conglomerate is actually wearing a uniform, it's just that it's jeans and a T-shirt, which half a century ago were symbols of free will and independence. It's confusing.

To try and make sense of this sartorial shift, this book will show you uniforms past and present, seek out the thinking behind them, and ask the fundamental question: why is it a good idea for people to look the same?

A uniform is a means of belonging and of making people belong. Nothing quite sums up the power of 'we' like a

uniform, and nothing quite so suppresses the potency of 'I'. If that thought seems disquieting, remember the upside: a uniform can create and engender within a body of people that complicated gung-ho concoction of pride and bonding that is best summed up by the phrase 'team spirit'. And that's not all: a good uniform can become the embodiment of its organization; it can even perform your recruitment job for you. Take sports, in which uniforms are called 'kit' or 'strip' in an attempt to make it all seem more fun. Generations of youngsters have grown up wearing the baseball caps of the New York Mets, or Manchester United football tops, dreaming that one day they might emulate their heroes and be wearing that familiar pinstripe or red for real.

Yet although they're part of a team, today's sportsmen become heroes in their own right, and so become individuals again. Players like Michael Jordan and David Beckham reached such celebrity status that they transcended the very teams they once considered the zenith of their aspirations. The 'I' became greater than the 'we'.

As uniformed sports stars take on the mantle of pop stars, they grow out of their uniforms and create their own. The Beckham boot and the Jordan Air Max trainer slipped into the public consciousness like a naughty schoolboy subtly modifying his uniform to show his independence from the school it embodies.

Why should this matter? We live in a world where individualism is ostensibly encouraged – it's self, self, self these days, isn't it? But for many of today's organizations – from schools to fast-food outlets to modern armies – individuality is chaos. They can't run on it. It's the sugar in their petrol. It gums up their works. The only way that they can operate is if many people come together and act as one. And if they can be made to look alike, it's the first step on the way to making them think and act alike. As American author and sociologist Philip Slater says, 'A person in a uniform is merely an extension of another person's will.'

To some extent a uniformed individual stops being a 'me' and starts being 'us' – 'us' being whichever organization

has persuaded him or her to wear it. This creates a number of feelings in the mind of the uniformed individual, from 'I belong' and 'I feel smart' to 'I want the next rank up' and 'I'm proud of the organization I work for'. Yet to the outside observer it signifies much more than this. It says 'there are more of us'; 'we are highly trained'; 'we take pride in our appearance'; 'we're better than you'; or even 'you can depend on us'.

To those supplying the uniform, it signifies organization. Indeed, uniforms have many hidden agendas – some we unconsciously accept all the time. Trust is a big factor here: if you hire a courier firm and hand over your important package to a spotty youth in jeans and a Misfits T-shirt, you'd be understandably concerned that it may not ever reach its destination. Dress this same pimply lad in a smart uniform and peaked cap and, although this is purely a cosmetic change, you are much more convinced. Recently, I was summoned to my bank to have a serious talk to them about money. I didn't expect frock coats and striped trousers but I was surprised to find it was a dress-down day 'for charity'. The manager and the entire staff were wearing jeans and sportswear. Now I'm a broad-minded kind of chap, and the bank has never (to my knowledge) mislaid one penny of my hard-earned capital, but I must confess that a certain mistrust crept into even my mind when dealing with a financial big cheese who looked ready for a barbecue rather than a board meeting.

Perhaps it's to be expected, though. These days it seems to be only the drones who wear uniforms. The more elaborate the uniform, the lower down the pecking order the poor prole wearing it actually seems to be. Conversely, the 'creatives' and the people who are so powerful that they don't need to care what other people think of them wear pretty much what they want.

Obviously, this has the potential to go badly wrong – one glance at the uniform polo shirts, chinos and deck shoes of the average dress-down Friday from Sydney to Seattle and you find yourself wishing that none of them had bothered. Some people need and crave the comfort of a uniform because they want to be like their boss, they don't want to stick their heads above the sartorial parapet, or because they have so much going on in their lives that they don't have time to sit on the bed in the morning debating the merits of whether a knitted tie goes with a floral shirt or a T-shirt goes with combat trousers. Einstein – a great individualist in his own right – got round this problem for much of his life by having exactly the same suit, tie and shirt for every day of the week.

We hope you enjoy this book, and whatever uniform you wear, we hope you're happy in it.

Previous left Nice work if you can get it: the Playboy Bunny garb was the first service uniform ever granted registration by the United States Patent and Trademark Office (patent number 762,884). In 1969 a larger white synthetic fur tail replaced the nylon one, apparently for 'better durability'.

Previous right Cary Grant wears a solar topee and still manages to look suave. The name of the headgear comes from the Hindi word *sola* (a type of plant used in its making) and *topi*, meaning hat. However, as it was used in hot climes to keep the sun off colonials' heads, the 'solar' name stuck.

Right Happy in his work: a butcher wearing the traditional striped apron and white hat.

1.MILITARY

1 MILITARY

Historians trace the rise of the uniform to 210BC, with the first emperor of China – Emperor Qin Shi Huang – who was laid to rest with an army of some 7,000 terracotta warriors to protect him. The armour and clothing of these soldiers vary according to rank but show real evidence of uniformity. Even their hairstyles, with the hair swept up to a small bun at the top of the head, are identikit. Meanwhile, on the other side of the globe, the Carthaginian general Hannibal (247–182BC) boasted an awesome battalion of uniformed troops. His Spanish mercenary infantry wore white tunics bordered with purple, and his elite Sacred Band of spearmen sported a white linen cuirass with a sunburst.

The rise of military uniforms stems from a number of requirements that remain as necessary today as they did two millennia ago. The heat of battle was a confusing and alarming place and the uniform ultimately provided a means by which combatants could be identified in a mêlée: just because you were fighting on the same side it did not necessarily follow that you would automatically distinguish your fellows from your enemy.

Anyone who doubts the power of a uniform should watch Sergio Leone's classic Western *The Good, the Bad and the Ugly*, set in the dog days of the American Civil War. 'Blondie' (Clint Eastwood) and his shifty but dim-witted associate Tuco, steal Confederate uniforms and meet an army marching towards them similarly clad in grey. Tuco waves and whoops for General Lee, shouting that God is with them and hates the Yankees, until the troops start to brush the desert dust off their clothes, revealing Union blue. 'God is not on our side,' mutters Blondie bitterly, 'because he hates idiots also.'

The rank system – shouting orders at juniors and thus the juniors' aspiration to shout orders at others still more junior than they – has been the way armies have worked for thousands of years. Rank and uniform have thus gone hand in hand, because uniform signifies status. The uniform was traditionally seen as a form of livery, so officers were slow to accept what they considered a demeaning servant's uniform, and would pay out of their own pockets for their own grand clothes. They dressed to show they weren't in this fighting game for the money but the glory, and their coats merely echoed the colours of their regiments. Eventually these dandies were forced to toe the line. Officers were ordered to wear uniform in the late eighteenth century and epaulettes – the tell-tale shoulder stripe that signifies a senior rank – were introduced into the British Army in 1768.

Uniforms helped to engender a feeling of pride in one's country and one's cause – charging into battle with similarly dressed compatriots unified fast-beating hearts and minds. We must not forget the view from the opposing ranks, either. Uniforms have long been a means of intimidating one's enemy by making soldiers appear taller, broader and generally more formidable than they would otherwise seem. King Frederick William I of Prussia was obsessed by making his troops appear as fearsome as possible and assembled three battalions of extremely tall men, whom he made even taller by their uniform of high mitre hats. 'Truly they are men supreme... the shortest of them rises, I think, towards seven feet, and some are nearly nine feet high,' wrote Thomas Carlyle, 1795–1881. He may have been exaggerating a little, but the Prussians certainly knew a thing or two about intimidation. They wore a version of the skull and crossbones, the *Totenkopf* or 'death's head', on their uniforms until well into the twentieth century (1918). The skull and crossbones has always served as a chilling reminder that the wearer means business, from the 'classic' flag of pirate Edward England in the eighteenth century to Nazi regiments such as the 5th Reiter Regiment who adopted it in 1921.

A uniform also leant the soldier a relative degree of safety, because a uniformed man was differentiated from a civilian bearing arms and hence afforded the protection of the regulations of war. And, should the combatant's courage fail him, a uniform also deterred desertion. A complex and unusual uniform could not be easily transformed into or blend in with civilian clothing.

One of the most important uses of the early uniform can be summed up simply: 'dress to impress'. Young men have always been peacocks and a great uniform makes it more desirable to sign up to an army – even when the chances of survival are slim. Even as late as 1914, the British Army found it easier to attract recruits to the rifle regiments (who wore a stylish dark green uniform) compared to the infantry. But let's not forget the reflected glory: in times when the commander of an army was required to kit out his troops from his own pocket, an impressive uniform reflected the glory back onto him.

Warfare in the eighteenth and nineteenth centuries was a colourful business – the British redcoats, the Austro-Hungarians' white tunics, the Swedes' blue and yellow. This was fine when armies fought with swords and inaccurate blunderbusses and cannons. However, by the end of the nineteenth century, the widespread use of the deadly accurate rifle brought an end to this spectrum of pugnacious popinjays.

The British had worn khaki since the days of the Indian uprising in 1857 – the word actually derives from the Hindi-Urdu word for 'dusty'. By 1902 they had developed a darker variant for European warfare, although they still retained their scarlet tunics for 'walking out'. The US Army adopted khaki the same year and the Danish Army produced a grey-green uniform a year later in 1903.

Previous page A Soviet soldier on parade in 1986 wearing a regimental red sash.

This page Two sailors aboard the USS New York, 1946. This publicity shot was intended to highlight the differences between the old type of Navy white dress uniform (right) and the new uniform (left). The changes included such radical ideas as 'shirt tucked into trousers'.

Khaki was soon taken up by nearly all the world's armies, apart from the French, who were still obstinately (and bravely) adhering to bright blue and red uniforms and old-fashioned headgear in battle as late as 1914. Other nations have kept their outlandish uniforms for ceremonial occasions. The Vatican's Swiss Guard sport striking Medici blues and yellows, while the 'fustanella' of the Greek Presidential Guard, or Evzones, is one of the most striking and unusual uniforms around.

The next logical advance from drab colours was to further blend in with your surroundings through camouflage. The German Nazi regime carried out much research into this subject and, in 1938, issued a four-colour *platanemuster* (plane tree) camouflage to units of the Waffen SS. Splinter pattern, palm, oak leaf and smoke variants all followed. They weren't the only ones: the Soviet Union issued an all-white camouflage for winter manoeuvres in 1938. The British continued to fight in drab, although in 1942 the camouflaged Denison smock was introduced. It was produced originally for the Parachute Regiment but was soon distributed more widely. Berets were introduced during World War II, initially in khaki, although regiments quickly chose different colours as a mark of pride and differentiation, including the famous maroon beret of the Parachute Regiment.

Khaki and camouflage are practical in battle but not necessarily impressive or smart. To retain some of the pomp of old-fashioned soldiery, many armies have taken to equipping their troops with several outfits for different occasions. The US Navy supplies its officers with white uniforms for warm weather, and their Marines still wear 'dress blues' – which include sky-blue trousers trimmed with red and white peaked caps – for ceremonial occasions. The British Household Cavalry's uniform of scarlet coat and peaked cap with plume has remained relatively unchanged since 1914.

As modern warfare uses science to think up 'smarter' ways of killing people, the soldier rarely actually sees the enemy, except via a computer screen and thermal-imaging camera. Thus military uniforms don't really need to be psychologically threatening to the enemy any more, although they still play a major part in troop morale. Modern army uniform is changing in the direction of practicality – it's time to look tough and fight dirty.

The uniform of the Greek Presidential Guards consists of a red baize hat with a silk tassel, a kilt of 30m of material and 400 pleats (symbolizing the years Greece was under Ottoman rule) and red leather shoes weighing 3kg that turn up to a point decorated with a black pompom. It can be traced back to the era of Homer and actually became the Greek national costume after the revolution in 1821.

The earliest evidence of a uniform: the Chinese Terracotta Army comprises over 7,000 models of soldiers that were placed to guard the body of the first emperor of China, Qin Shi Huang, in 210BC.

Opposite Alexander the Great (born 356BC) wore shining armour and white plumes in his hat to distinguish him from the uniforms of his rank and file soldiers. When not in battle he would often be seen wearing silk in the royal colours of purple and white.

This page A Japanese samurai warrior in traditional armour wielding the *katana*, or longsword. Sword making in Japan took off in the tenth century due to techniques brought over from China with increasing trade.

Above Ancient versus modern. A samurai on horseback is followed by modern Japanese tanks. The headgear and the body armour of 1,000 years ago has a definite influence on modern battle armour.

Opposite Three samurai in armour. A male child would receive his sword and armour in a ceremony called *genbuku* on his 13th birthday.

The uniform's power to depersonalize and impress. The North Korean Army parades in its thousands in Pyongyang, 2005. Even the crowd is well-drilled, holding their coloured placards with military precision.

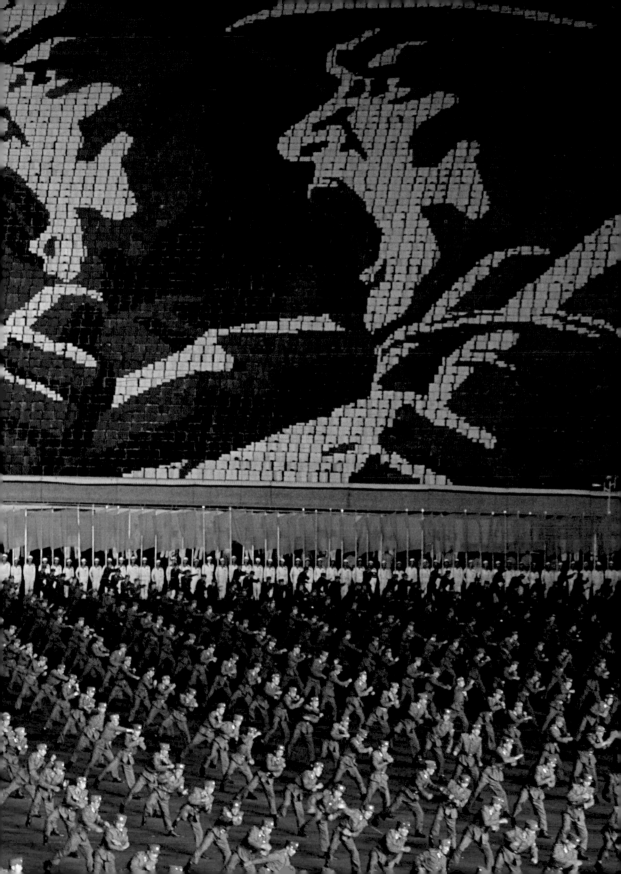

Opposite Napoleon Joseph Charles Bonaparte (one of the many 'Napoleons' of the Bonaparte family) in uniform, 1855. The epaulettes give emphasis to the shoulders and the three-quarter length buttoned coat gives gravitas, emphasizing his height, which was never a strong point with the Bonaparte clan.

Above The Confederate Army in grey fighting the Republican Army in Union blue during the American Civil War (1861–65).

Above Sailors in the Russian Navy demonstrate incredible precision in their drill. Their marching is so tight that their uniforms produce solid blocks of colour and pattern.

Opposite A medal presentation on the British Royal Navy's HMS *Invincible* is rendered slightly less solemn by the wearing of tropical uniform of white shorts and long socks.

Left The last German emperor and King of Prussia, Kaiser Wilhelm II in spectacular full hussar uniform, c.1910. He had a fearsome temper, and once, in a 1908 interview with the *Daily Telegraph*, said, 'You English are mad, mad, mad as March hares.'

Opposite German pre-Nazi uniform had its roots in the ceremonial dress of World War I.

Above Medals conferred on a member of the 2nd Armoured Division of General Leclerc, whose men liberated Paris on 25 August 1944.

Opposite, top left American air ace Richard Bong with his P-38 Lightning 'Marge' and aircrew. By World War II, pilots' uniforms had made huge advances in practicality. Aircrews wore leather flight jackets to keep out the intense cold at altitude and, when back at base, chinos for comfort.

Opposite, bottom left British pilots in flying helmets housing radio communication equipment. A collar and tie was also worn to keep things smart and military.

Opposite, bottom right A studio portrait of a British RAF pilot c.1945. Note his thick gauntlets, boots and goggles – unpressurized aircraft were extremely cold. The air force had a reputation for being the most lax of the armed forces, which is perhaps why he has been able to get away with a drawing of his girlfriend on his flight vest.

Left Adolf Hitler on the Eastern Front in 1941. Compared with the uniform excesses for which the Nazis are remembered, Hitler is seen wearing a remarkably ordinary combat jacket teamed with white shirt and black tie.

Japanese kamikaze pilots from World War II in flying suits and air helmets. By the end of the war, the Japanese naval air service had sacrificed over 2,500 pilots on suicide missions.

Below Manfred von Richthofen, the most successful flying ace of World War I with over 80 victories to his name, poses by his Fokker Dr1 Triplane. Air combat was a new phenomenon in the early twentieth century, and these original air warriors wore a uniform that echoed that of land-based cavalry soldiering, including tight knee-length boots, jodhpurs and a buttoned jacket.

Opposite A German Luftwaffe pilot in the cockpit of his Messerschmitt, 1942. The blue-grey uniform echoes that of his counterparts in the British RAF, while the German cap appeared in many formats, notably the standard Waffen-SS enlisted overseas cap, featuring a death's head on the front.

American World War II sailor mechanics refuel an SNC advanced training plane at Texas' Corpus Christi naval air base, 1942. Their distinctive 'Dixie cup' white caps mark them out as men of the seafaring forces.

Opposite A novel method of standing to attention: a South Korean soldier stands with legs spread wide and biceps flexed. If the posture weren't enough, the helmet and regulation dark glasses enhance the intimidating effect.

This page Young Chinese border soldiers patrolling the Turugart Pass, 1996. Despite China's historical lack of communication with the West, these peaked caps, fatigues and belted forage jackets with epaulettes appear to be inspired by the uniforms of Western armies.

This page A member of the Bosnian regiment within the Croatian Army, allied with Germany, during World War II, c.1941. The distinctive maroon fez was an integral part of the uniform, and worn by Muslim volunteers and German officers alike.

Opposite, top A female soldier in the Moroccan Army wears lavish maroon parade dress during the first anniversary of the coronation of Mohammed VI, 2000. The white peaked cap and gold shoulder tassels mark this outfit as a purely ceremonial uniform.

Opposite, bottom A candid shot of a female soldier from the US 48th Brigade Combat Team during a farewell departure ceremony at Fort Stewart, Georgia, USA. Her forage cap and camouflage combat jacket are identical to those of her male comrades.

Right Ukrainian female paratroopers
watch during training at the shooting-
range. More than 20,000 women serve
in the Ukrainian armed forces, making
up about 10 per cent of the country's
total military strength.

Left It must be hard to march in tight skirts but these Indonesian women soldiers struggle bravely on despite uniform restrictions during a ceremony to commemorate the 59th anniversary of the country's armed forces in Jakarta, 2004.

Opposite Chelsea pensioners in their smart red coats and striking tricorne cocked hats, used for ceremonial occasions. The coat refers back to the famous red coat worn by many regiments of the British Army in the eighteenth century. The pensioners are all long-serving soldiers or those that have been injured in service.

Above US Marines exercise on board the USS *Kearsarge* in the Adriatic Sea wearing standard-issue olive drab T-shirts and shorts teamed with distinctly non-military training shoes.

The Swiss Guard at the Vatican in their striking Medici blue, red and yellow. This full dress uniform has remained relatively unchanged since the seventeenth century, although their everyday uniform is in a simpler plain blue.

Opposite French Foreign Legion soldiers drum in formation at a parade in front of the gates of the Legion's headquarters in Sidi Bel Abbès, Algeria, 1940. Very little of the uniform has changed in nearly 70 years. The rounded white peaked cap, or kepi, was first worn in 1907 and has become associated with the French Foreign Legion. The original was khaki but tended to bleach through washing and after prolonged exposure to the sun.

Above left A Foreign Legion standard bearer in Algeria, 1940. The red shoulder epaulettes of this parade costume are designed to emphasize the width of the shoulders, while the white gauntlets and 'Sam Brown' belt would be completely inappropriate in anything other than formal parade attire.

Above Foreign Legionnaires parade in Paris on Bastille Day, 14th July, 2007. The white kepi hat and red tasselled shoulder ornamentation have persisted unchanged since the 1940s.

Left The German Army has always been at the forefront of camouflage technology – even prior to World War II. A heavily camouflaged Luftwaffe sniper in 2006 has his face and hands (the two most readily distinguished areas in battle) completely covered.

Above Britain's Prince Harry perfects the art of jungle camouflage so that few enemies would recognize him or realize he is actually third in line to the throne.

Camouflage has progressed enormously from the early attempts by the German SS during World War II. This modern soldier cleverly blends in with his background.

2.AUTHORITY

2 AUTHORITY

In the year 2000 the city of Buenos Aires was considering ways of attracting members of the transgender community into the police force. One of the major obstacles was the uniform. 'We did a fact-finding survey of the community,' said chief commissioner Raoul Bronson, 'it brought back one overwhelming response, "Sorry, but we wouldn't be seen dead in those uniforms!"'

Today's accelerated global communication means we're more style-conscious than ever before. And that means that whatever we do, we just won't accept bad uniforms. Whether you work as a traffic warden, a policeman or a security guard, your uniform is a point of pride and has a distinct bearing on your morale. In the summer of 2007, Thai police chiefs utilized this trait as a disciplinarian tactic, and officers who turned up late or committed other small offences were made to wear armbands featuring the popular Japanese cartoon character 'Hello Kitty'. 'It's not something macho police officers want covering their biceps,' explained Colonel Pongpat Chayaphan, stating the obvious '... it will make them feel guilt, and prevent them from repeating the offence.'

It seems hard to believe, but the concept of 'police' is not yet 200 years old. The first true police force was established by the British home secretary Robert Peel in 1829. The early forces needed a mark of authority because the public was not yet used to the idea of being ordered around by policemen, and because the only weapon they had was a truncheon. Each of the 144 constables was equipped with a long, dark blue coat and a tall top hat capable of bearing the bobby's weight if he needed to peer over walls. The choice of coat colour was important. Blue was chosen for its associations with the Royal Navy, since sailors were seen by the man in the street as heroes, and to differentiate the police from British soldiers, who wore red coats and were generally loathed by the public for breaking up protests brutally.

The concept of a police force spread around the world and soon a myriad of troopers, sheriffs, rangers and 'peace officers' were established to uphold the law and keep the peace. With them came specific uniforms designed for the purpose, all of which had some military influence. Like the soldier, a policeman needs to stand out and inspire respect. Uniforms promote discipline and pride in one's appearance. They are also functional – the standard bell-shaped British policeman's 'custodian' helmet was based on the Prussian military helmet, and introduced in the 1860s to ward off blows from blackguard's cudgels. It has become a symbol of England to tourists, who can still buy plastic replicas from London street stalls.

The red serge jackets and fawn Stetsons of the Royal Canadian Mounted Police, or Mounties, have become one of the most recognized police uniforms in the world, although now they are only worn for formal occasions. The Mounties were conceived by Canada's first prime minister, Sir John A. Macdonald, in an attempt to bring law and order to the Northwest Territories, which were awash with tough, hard-bitten prospectors who were in turn awash with a plentiful supply of strong whiskey from America.

America's Californian Highway Patrol uniform also boasts the Stetson. The uniform usually consists of a light khaki shirt with a badge featuring the goddess Minerva (for wisdom) and khaki trousers with a blue and gold stripe. However, thanks to the popular 1970s television series *CHiPs*, it's the police motorcycle cops who stand out in the public consciousness, with cool accessories such as Ray-Ban aviator sunglasses and knee-length boots.

In the cities of the twenty-first century, we accept almost subconsciously that anyone wearing a uniform must be in a position of authority. We follow their orders with a grumble but without a question. 'You can't go down there' or, 'You can't park there', they say, and we just mutter under our breath and get on with our daily commute. This has led to some unfortunate incidents: in crime-rife Mexico City in 2003 you could buy a fake police uniform on the street and get up to any amount of nefarious practices. The city's police chief, Marcelo Ebrard was forced to keep one step ahead of the criminal element by issuing new hi-tech uniforms that were harder to copy. Simple subterfuge works during wartime too: some members of the Taleban in Afghanistan have also been known to attack American Special Forces while disguised as local police.

Today's police uniforms have both softened and hardened with the times. The modern police officer is expected to communicate and empathize with society, so many forces have abandoned overbearing militaristic uniforms in favour of pullovers and caps instead of helmets. However, some countries – southeast Asia in particular – still prefer their police to look formidable. To the Western observer, the Vietnamese police could be mistaken for the army. City streets the world over are increasingly dangerous places and urban police are often seen sporting stab-proof vests and body armour. This duality gives modern uniform designers an ever more difficult job in finding the right balance between respect, empathy and functionality.

Outside of the police forces most uniforms seen on our city streets still borrow heavily from the military look. This is because we unconsciously associate the soldierly look with authority and if, for example, you're a traffic warden slapping fines on the cars of belligerent motorists, then you need every inch of authority that you can muster.

THE HENLEY COLLEGE LIBRARY

Previous page Iranian police 'calm down' protesting students outside the British Embassy in Tehran. Their protective helmets also feature neck guards to afford limited defence in the event of attacks from the rear.

This page John Travolta in his civil aircraft pilot's uniform. The bars on the sleeve indicate that he is an airline pilot and Travolta has indeed clocked up over 5,000 hours at the joystick since gaining his wings in 1974.

However, you don't have to be in a position of authority to experience the uniform's influence on our clothes. Our casual jackets have epaulettes, and even the humble T-shirt started life as part of a uniform. Referring to the 'T' shape it made when laid out flat, it was first seen in the 1930s as an item of underwear for the USC (University of Southern California) football team. During World War II the shirt was issued to the US Army and Navy as part of the uniform. Although it was technically designed as a piece of underwear, soldiers often wore it on its own when exercising or performing arduous sweaty tasks.

Post-war 1950s American cinema cemented the deal for the T-shirt. The role models were Marlon Brando in 1953's *The Wild One* and James Dean in 1955's *Rebel Without A Cause*. The T-shirt found its other function – advertising – as early as 1948, when presidential candidate Thomas E. Dewey produced a 'Dew it for Dewey' T-shirt, followed closely by 1952 candidate Dwight D. Eisenhower, who had an 'I Like Ike' T-shirt made.

The war-torn twentieth century meant military uniforms – or what we know today as 'army surplus' – were plentiful and, by the 1960s had found a whole new generation that was anarchic and impertinent enough to wear them, attracting mixed reactions from those who had actually fought in the war. The Beatles' 1967 album, *Sgt. Pepper's Lonely Hearts Club Band*, showed the group in psychedelic uniform, but to really understand how outrageous this was, you only have to chuckle over Ringo Starr's cheeky comment to a representative of the older generation in Richard Lester's film *A Hard Day's Night*, three years earlier:

Outraged man on train: I fought the war for your sort!
Ringo: Bet you're sorry you won!

The Beatles' *Sgt. Pepper's Lonely Hearts Club Band* album cover, designed by English pop artist Peter Blake. The band wanted to look like they were a military marching band who'd just come off a bandstand in a suburban park. The yellow, pink, turquoise and red uniforms show evidence of 1960s subversion.

Left The British policeman's uniform had remained virtually unchanged since the 1950s, although by the 1970s they were allowed to grow their hair long, just as the rest of the world was getting into punk.

Above A British policeman guarding the Houses of Parliament with automatic machine gun and Kevlar body armour.

Above The Chinese police were issued with new 'Style 99' special uniforms in 2007, including regular-issue clothing, seen here, and combat uniforms. In an attempt to smarten up the force prior to the 2008 Olympic Games, new rules forbidding dyed hair, long hair, shaven heads or facial hair were brought in.

Opposite New York Port Authority police officers with machine guns patrol the British Airways and United Airlines terminal at John F. Kennedy International Airport, New York, USA, 2006. Their functional uniform comprises peaked forage caps and black combats. Black in policing terms has gradually replaced navy blue worldwide, and tends to signify that you mean business – and they do.

The US television series *CHiPS* ran for 139 episodes and starred, from left to right, Erik Estrada, Larry Wilcox and Robert Pine. Because of the Californian heat, their uniform paid scant attention to motorcycle safety, relying on only a tight beige shirt and trousers and open-faced helmet. Ray-Ban aviator sunglasses were an essential part of the outfit.

Above Spanish police on parade wear blue serge jackets with epaulettes and brass buttons and belt detailing. The hats are tight-fitting and their pillbox shape, flaring at the back, is borrowed from traditional Spanish dress. Similar shaped hats are also worn by toreadors.

Opposite A state trooper from Utah, America. The Stetson is a ubiquitous form of headgear in American policing, and is an icon of American life. John B. Stetson first began making his classic 'Boss of the Plains' hat in 1865.

Opposite In Shaanxi Province, China, law enforcement officers jog through the streets of Xian during the Law Enforcement Torch Run for the 2007 Special Olympics. Their uniform of black forage cap, short-sleeved shirt and functional boots is perfect for intense physical exertion like this.

Above Italian military police dog handlers wearing dark berets and olive drab combat jackets. The dogs don't wear a uniform, but are of a uniform breed – Alsatians.

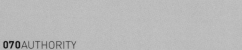

Opposite The uniform of the modern Californian Highway Patrolman, with its boots and tight, jodhpur-like trousers with black piping has much in common with equestrianism.

Above Jordan's famous Desert Patrol send their Camel Corps where four-wheel-drive vehicles can't go. Their uniform is a melange of military styling (long, green serge coats) and traditional Arab dress. The distinctive red and white headscarf, or *shemagh*, has been worn in the desert for centuries.

Field Marshall Montgomery in the duffel coat, an item that symbolized his no-nonsense approach to leadership and the strong bond he had with his men. Post-war, this distinctive warm toggled coat was favoured by beatniks, students and even Paddington Bear.

Previous page, left Idi Amin was one of the world's most feared and unpredictable dictators, ruling Uganda from 1971 until 1979. He even designed a special uniform for himself – well, no one was going to argue with him. He also awarded himself many medals based on English ones, including the 'Victorious Cross', which copied the Commonwealth's famous Victoria Cross for bravery.

Previous page, right General Pinochet was president of Chile from 1974 to 1990. His uniform here would not be out of place at a Nazi SS convention. No stranger to uniform, he became general and then commander-in-chief of the military, paving his way to power.

Opposite, top Thai Police ready for action in motorcycle-style helmets and fingerless gloves, which promote manual dexterity when using firearms and also offer some protection.

Opposite, bottom Whether you call it peacekeeping or world policing, the United Nations troops, with their characteristic blue berets, have seen a sixfold rise since 1998 and are sent into some of the world's toughest situations.

Above Spanish Guardia Civil have a mainly military function: guarding buildings, national security and crowd control. Their green serge uniforms reflect this and are military in appearance to distinguish them from the municipal and local police.

Above Taken from one of the final scenes in *Casablanca*, this still shows Humphrey Bogart in military trench coat and Hollywood's take on uniform with that of police captain Renault (middle).

Opposite Not even the rich can escape the power of the traffic warden. The concept began in the UK in 1958 with the introduction of the parking meter. The wardens were immediately detested and motorists did not give them the respect they would a policeman. Issuing wardens with a smart uniform and peaked cap implied authority.

This page You wouldn't argue with these Vietnamese traffic wardens – their quasi-military regalia instantly lends them respect of which their Western counterparts can only dream.

Opposite These British traffic wardens patrolling the streets of Keynsham, Bristol, wear a very male uniform of tie, dark trousers and fleece. The introduction of the light, man-made fleece fibre has transformed many modern uniforms.

Brixton Tulse Hill

This page The passing of the Routemaster bus (seen here in 1995) has been a sad loss to London's streets, not least because more modern buses are no longer patrolled by the well-loved conductors, who dispensed help and information along with tickets. Their uniform of smart blazer and tie enhanced their respect.

Opposite These train conductors from 1910 wear smart peaked caps and military jackets designed to demonstrate their authority to fare-paying (and fare-dodging) passengers.

This page A study in scarlet as The Royal Canadian Mounted Police parade in their distinctive red coats and fawn Stetsons. The colour is just for show – in real-life policing the Mounties wear standard police wear and horses are not used on operations by any unit.

Opposite A Scottish bagpiper wearing full military uniform including bearskin hat, tartan cloak and kilt and sporran. The Scoti, who settled in Western Scotland from the fifth century, used striped garments to signify rank. The word tartan derives from the Irish *tarsna* (crosswise) and the early Scottish Gaelic *tarsuinn* (across).

Above Johnny Depp and Geoffrey Rush in *Pirates of the Caribbean*. Pirate captains were indeed dandies who picked clothes from those they had overpowered in battle – belts, long coats and frilled shirts. However, on board ship most pirates would have worn simpler clothes in order to facilitate movement.

Opposite, top A drum majorette practises twirling her baton at Freeport, Long Island, USA. The majorette costume has taken the most upbeat aspects of military life – popinjay uniforms and marching – and has dispensed with the more distasteful ones, namely war and fighting.

Opposite, bottom A Marine drummer in Parris Island, South Carolina, USA, 1942. His ceremonial parade outfit of scarlet cross-buttoned coat and white cap and trousers was later to influence non-military majorettes.

Opposite, top left The majorette of the Kansas Jayhawks leads the band during the game against the Kansas State Wildcats at Memorial Stadium on November 18, 2006 in Lawrence, Kansas, USA. The short buttoned jacket and headgear owe a great deal to military influence.

Opposite, top right A trumpeter from the West Virginia Marching Band during the game between the West Virginia Mountaineers and the East Carolina Pirates at Milan Puskar Stadium in Morgantown, West Virginia, USA, 2007. Although completely non-military, the sash, cape and helmet trimmed with feathers all betray a military lineage.

Opposite, bottom The Malcolm X Shabazz Marching Band from Newark, New Jersey, USA. The band has performed for former president Clinton and the school is 95 per cent African American.

Below Kilted bagpipers participate in 'The Nation's Parade' November 10, 1995, in New York City, USA, a tribute to the eight million men and women who served the United States, at home and abroad, during World War II.

A town crier in St George, Bermuda. The traditional role (and uniform) was carried overseas to British colonies.

The role of the English town crier can be traced back to 1066, when levels of literacy were low or non-existent among the average population and the crier was relied upon to proclaim the news of the day from the town square. Such an important figure had to stand out, and the traditional garb of tricorne hat trimmed with ostrich feathers, red and gold coat, bell and breeches rendered him instantly identifiable as the man with the news. This picture was taken in Hastings, East Sussex, in 2002.

This page A Yeoman Warder of Her Majesty's Royal Palace and Fortress the Tower of London, also known as a Beefeater. The scarlet and gold dress uniform dates from 1552 and is worn only on state occasions.

Opposite In 2007, Yeoman Warder Moira Cameron became the first female Beefeater in the history of the Tower of London. The black uniform with red piping dates back to 1485, when the first Beefeaters patrolled the parapets and passageways of the Tower, protecting the Crown Jewels.

Above and right Barristers wearing traditional dress in Hong Kong, 1997. The wigs worn by barristers are in the style favoured in the late eighteenth century, when they adopted the garb as a token of mourning for the death of Queen Anne in 1714.

Opposite, top Judges gather at the State Opening of Parliament, Westminster Palace, London, 1985, wearing wigs and ceremonial crimson robes trimmed with ermine.

Opposite, bottom French public prosecutor Henri Desclaux and prosecuting attorney Marc Robert in Bordeaux, Aquitaine, 1998. Their red robes trimmed with ermine echo those of their British counterparts.

Above Queen Elizabeth II and Prince
Philip, Duke of Edinburgh at the House of
Lords in London for the State Opening of
Parliament. The Queen wears formal white
with a crimson cape and train, while her
consort wears his military medals. The two
pageboys to the left wear traditional garb
of ruff, buttoned coat, buckled shoes and
knickerbockers.

Opposite Michael Berry Savory, Lord
Mayor of the City of London 2004–05
in traditional robes, chain of office and
tricorne hat at a service to mark the 200th
anniversary of Nelson's victory at Trafalgar,
2005. The first recorded Mayor of London
was Henry Fitz-Ailwyn, 1189, although
the outfit's origins only date to the
fifteenth century.

Parliament members dressed in traditional Moroccan clothes await the arrival of King Mohammed VI prior to the opening parliament session in Rabat, Morocco, 2003. The origins of the hooded *jellaba* lie in practicality – it is a very cool garment in hot countries.

This page The newly appointed Archbishop of Warsaw, Stanislaw Wielgus, adjusts his mitre during mass. In the Roman Catholic church the right to wear the mitre is confined to bishops and abbots.

Opposite Pope Benedict XVI attends a meeting with Italian President Carlo Azeglio Ciampi in the papal library of the Apostolic Palace in Vatican City on 3 May 2005. His bright red Papal slippers are actually a historical vestment of the Roman Catholic Church. The colour symbolizes the blood of the martyrs, and the wearer's submission to the ultimate authority of Jesus Christ.

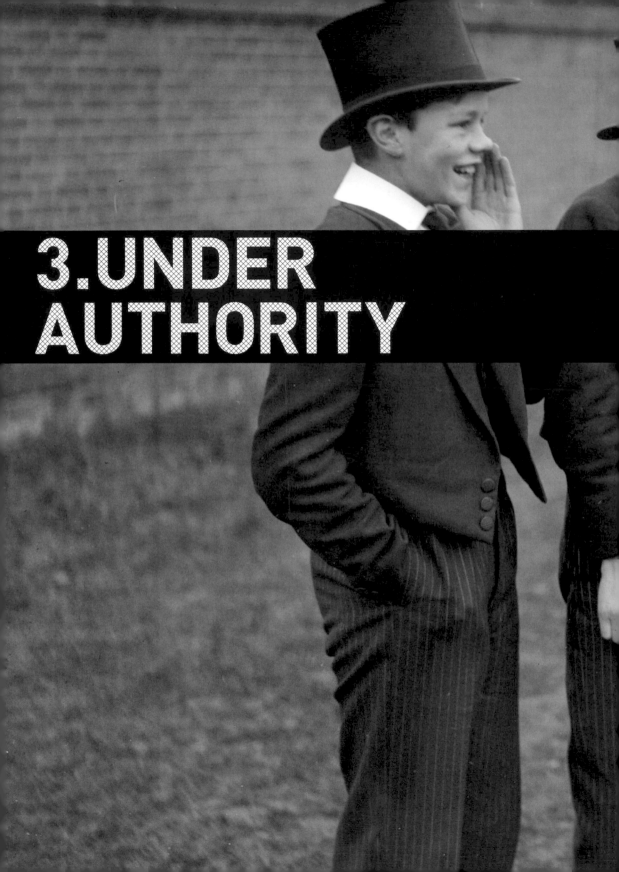

3.UNDER
AUTHORITY

3 UNDER AUTHORITY

In the 1960s school uniforms were seen by many modern-thinking educationalists as an unnecessary frippery on the edge of the real business of schooling. However, remove a uniform from a school and problems quickly emerge.

One of the most cited reasons in favour of a school uniform is as a means of discipline and control. This belief tends to reside mainly in the mind of the schoolteacher looking out on a playground full of similarly clad pupils. The pupils themselves tend to resent the uniform until they are given the option of not wearing it, when the problem of the schoolyard fashion faux pas rears its ugly head.

A school uniform performs a democratizing function – children with bad or unfashionable clothes don't need to worry about being bullied or picked on. Sometimes a uniform is a blessing because it prevents agonizing minutes deciding what to wear in the morning. I'd also argue that a school uniform, rather than stifling the imagination, promotes creativity, because the blank canvas of a school uniform encourages kids' innate ability to rebel. At my school we were constantly at war with the edicts of official uniform, getting our trousers taken in to ridiculous drainpipe-thin widths, tying our ties the wrong way round so they looked modishly narrow, or knotting them in ridiculously fat Windsors. We'd buy winkle-picker shoes that were officially banned, grow our hair long if short hair was required, or shave it off completely if a certain length was stipulated. The late 1980s meant hair dye was de rigueur, even though it was the most obvious transgression of school rules. It was a constant running battle with authority, but I'd like to think that fashion and style were the victors.

With so many inventive, rebellious young brains around, the idea that you can make children 'uniform' is never going to be a completely achievable goal. Even the strictest public schools realize this and dangle sartorial individualism as a carrot on a stick to encourage pupils to try harder. At England's most famous public school, Eton, prefects are allowed to stand out from fellow pupils in fancy waistcoats and grey trousers. Flashy house ties are still awarded for excellence in sports in many schools, and at my minor English public school in the northwest of England, the school rules still stated that the head boy was allowed to grow a beard (if he could, or indeed wished to), smoke a pipe and keep a dog!

Another factor in favour of school uniform is that of identification and fostering pride in your school. From personal experience I can say that these emotions were only stirred up when engaging other schools in the regular pitched battles that used to take place on certain hotly contested boundaries. And so they attained the status of

military uniform. This sense of adult organization was highlighted and exaggerated to comic effect in the *St Trinian's* films of the 1950s and 1960s, where the boaters and pinafores of the seemingly beautifully turned out schoolgirls concealed criminal masterminds and hellcats who were fascinated by adult vices such as robbery and gambling.

From a historical perspective, after the fall of the Roman Empire schooling in the West was patchy to say the least, and so were the uniforms. *The Village School*, painted by the Dutch artist Jan Steen in the mid-seventeenth century portrays a chaotic classroom with children wearing peasant outfits of different hues and shapes. The only school uniforms to speak of were religious in their origin. In the fourteenth century Islamic *medersas* or holy schools were created, like the Ben Youssef Medersa in Morocco's Marrakesh. Pupils had to wear the long gowns (*izar* and *reda*) and skullcap (*kufi*) of Muslim clerics.

Meanwhile, in the West, uniforms were first seen at the English 'hospital schools' of the Tudor period. These 'poor' schools were also known as 'bluecoat schools', due to the long, cassock-like blue coats the boys wore (and still do) because they were founded by religious institutions. These blue coats, teamed with knee breeches and stockings, were first seen at Christ's Hospital School in London. Many other bluecoat schools sprang up across Britain, including Chetham's Hospital School in Manchester and The Blue Coat School in Liverpool.

In contrast to the charity schools, English public schools for the wealthy of the eighteenth and nineteenth centuries were lawless places where pupils could wear and do pretty much whatever they liked. The reformation of these establishments in the late nineteenth century to produce new young Empire builders led to the introduction of uniforms in an attempt to combat the chaos and introduce discipline. Academically selective grammar schools followed for poorer, gifted pupils, and these took up the concept of the uniform as a way of emphasizing their excellence. Thus school uniform, which began its life as a sign of poverty, came to signify both higher social class and high educational aspirations.

Other nations soon copied. From 1867, the Meiji era saw Japanese schools model themselves on French and German academic values. Japan introduced Western-style school uniforms in the late nineteenth century and they have remained an integral part of school life. In countries like Malaysia, school uniforms are divided on religious grounds: Muslim girls wear a long knee-length blouse, the *baju kurung*, whereas non-Muslims wear pinafores.

Many schools have developed a unique style of dress – Harrow has its boater hats and Eton has its short

Previous page 'Play up, play up and play the game!' Public schoolboys at Eton, wearing the classic garb of top hats, pinstriped trousers and short 'bumfreezer' jackets, watch their classmates playing the Wall Game, traditionally played between town and school on St Andrew's Day.

This page Classic junior school outfit of shorts, long socks and black pumps. He's holding conkers behind his back, or a frog.

'bumfreezer' jackets and top hats. However, some countries have never really taken up school uniforms in a big way. German pupils wore blue coats (blue being the cheapest dye around) until the late 1700s, but school uniforms were not prevalent, except in public schools, and student hats were banned by the Nazis for being too class-driven.

The distinguished academic gown and mortarboard hat was inspired by ecclesiastical dress. European universities were very much extensions of the church; it was only as late as 1858 that the British law was repealed that required university dons to be in Holy Orders. The habits the monks wore became modified to identify their universities, while the mortarboard hat was developed from the skullcap worn by monks and churchmen in the sixteenth century. Once worn by the majority of schoolmasters (see the 1939 film *Goodbye, Mr Chips*) it is now largely an anachronism, although it is still worn by some public schoolteachers, university professors and by graduating students.

At Oxford, caps, gowns and white bow ties are still worn for enrolment, and frequently for formal dinners and examinations. In the United States the tassel on the mortar board has developed a significance of its own, being colour coordinated to the discipline in which the student is graduating, for example crimson for journalism and brown for the arts. It's worth adding that the imagery behind the highly successful *Harry Potter* film series draws on the rites, rituals and clothes of the English boarding school, with the pupils of Hogwarts wearing wizards' cloaks that resemble academic gowns.

In this chapter you'll see all manner of uniforms forced upon people in an attempt to subdue and control them.

Prisoners wearing the classic striped uniform (to assist identification of escapees) being drilled by a guard in 1910.

Girls' school uniforms from around the world.

Opposite, clockwise from top left
Smart blue blazer and beret combination; blazer worn with straw boater hat for summer uniform; trainers replace plimsolls as school everyday footwear; and a smart trouser and neckerchief combination from the USA.

This page A businesslike but simple tartan pinafore and plaits.

Boarding schoolboys from St Bede's Preparatory School in Kent, England, dig into some tuck on the train down to start another term, 1947. The grey flannel cloth used for the blazers and shorts was designed to be as hard-wearing as possible to withstand the rigours of schoolboy life.

Pupils from Hill House School in Knightsbridge, central London, in their distinctive uniform of brown knickerbockers and tan vests. The uniform lacks a tie and is designed for physical activity as well as lessons. The wife of the school's founder is reported as saying, 'A grey uniform produces grey minds.'

The way a tie is worn can make or break the gravitas of a school uniform, identifying the wearer as a conformer or a rebel. Compare the mode of neckwear tying of the schoolboys (**opposite**) and the girl on the right (**this page**) and you just know who's going to be in detention this week.

Opposite Even though they are supposed to sidestep fashion, school uniforms have always been subject to the prevailing style of the day. These two teenagers turn the collar of their blazers up to add their own tweak to conformity.

Right International menswear designers spend years working out how to get that indefinable sense of cool across in their adverts. And then some schoolboys just put on a blazer, undo their top button and achieve it instantly.

This page These Japanese schoolgirls have a uniform that is a veritable melange of diverse cultural statements, from the cricket-style sweater to the tartan kilt-style skirts. The blazers, with their brass buttons, have their roots in naval uniforms.

Opposite Whatever the uniform, children will always find a way to bend the rules and personalize it. Here, Japanese schoolgirls give their smart blazers a modern twist with dancers' baggy legwarmers.

Opposite In this scene from the 1939 film *Goodbye, Mr Chips*, the eponymous hero wears a mortarboard and gown and his students wear top hats, indicating the film's Etonian influence.

Above Eton College has developed a reputation for prestige and privilege that is second to none, but until the 1960s, there were actually no official school dress regulations. The suits the pupils wore were completely dictated by fashion and, more importantly, peer pressure.

Among university students the mortarboard and gown are now largely only worn upon graduation. The gown's origins date back to medieval Europe when universities were usually linked to monasteries, hence students had to wear clerical dress.

This page Two Chinese Pioneers hold the red flag aloft wearing olive drab uniforms. The Young Pioneer movement is now the largest youth organization in the world, involving children in Russia, Eastern Europe, China, Cuba, North Korea and Vietnam for nearly half a century. The uniform often varies from country to country, but the bonding item of uniform is the red scarf.

Opposite American scouts showing the many varieties of uniform that have developed from Baden-Powell's original brief.

Opposite, top Actor Alec Baldwin poses for a photo with girl scouts and boy scouts during the 'Proud to be an American' softball game to benefit the New York State World Trade Center Relief Fund September 22, 2001 in Amagansett, New York State, USA.

Opposite, bottom left A Palestinian scout bangs the drum for President Yasser Arafat. Scout founder Baden-Powell stipulated the neckerchief, which can be pressed into many uses including acting as a sun protector and to keep dust out of the nose and mouth.

Opposite, bottom right The distinctive neckerchief is the main feature of this scout's uniform.

Left Scouting is a truly international movement: Hezbullah scouts perform drills in southern Lebanon, July 2000.

Below Cub scouts, the junior branch of scouting, in relaxed mode. Their uniform is similar to the scouts' but has traditionally been worn with shorts. The trousers are definitely non-standard issue. What would Baden-Powell have said?

Not a Hells Angels' rally but a scout jamboree.

This page A mature scout wears uniform (tweaked with bandana and shades) at the 2007 World Scout Jamboree in Chelmsford, England.

Opposite Scouts in a melange of shorts, baseball caps and jungle hats (but always with the neckerchief and woggle) march at the 2007 World Scout Jamboree.

Religious vestments have historically served a dual purpose: to show the wearer's obeisance to a deity while also elevating the wearer from the masses and emphasizing their religious authority or vocation.

Opposite, top Monks in Myanmar's Shan province wear their simple lifestyle proudly – shaved heads, bare feet and brown robes.

Opposite, bottom left Austrian monks wearing more dressy robes during study in their manuscript room.

Opposite, bottom right Polish monks in Krakow wear simple habits originating from the fourteenth century and jarring slightly with the mobile phone.

This page Nuns wearing the distinctive headgear of the Missionaries of Charity assemble at Saint Mary's Church in Calcutta, India, on 15th August 2001 to witness the official closing ceremony on the enquiry into the life of the late Mother Teresa.

The vestments of altarboys and choirboys lend gravitas to the wearers and disguise what might otherwise be the usual schoolboy disorder.

Opposite, top A Catholic ceremony in Cologne, Germany.

Opposite, bottom The choir sing Christmas carols at King's College, Cambridge, England.

Left A Christmas ceremony at the Church of St Catherine, Bethlehem.

Below A procession of French Benedictine monks at Bec Abbey, France.

Laurel and Hardy in prison uniforms
in *Liberty*, 1929. The US prisoner's
wardrobe was intended to be as
distinctive as possible to deter escape –
not that it had any effect on Stan and
Ollie. Stripes or arrows were often
employed to make the escapee stand out.

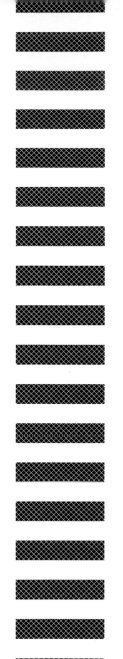

Whatever the colour, prison uniform must be distinctive, durable and easy to manufacture. Prison garb is a way of keeping inmates in check, both psychologically and practically. It reinforces the fact that the inmate is 'in the system' while also making it harder to blend in with the outside world should he or she attempt to escape.

Left to right A US prisoner in blue; the yellow of Salt Lake County Jail, Utah; America's first female chain-gang in bright orange at Maricopa County Prison, Phoenix, Arizona.

A white uniform is issued to prisoners from the Limestone Correctional Facility, Alabama, 1995. The practice of chaining prisoners together to form a chain-gang had not been seen in America for 30 years prior to this.

Guantanamo Bay detainees are given bright orange jumpsuits and flip-flops in a modern take on prison wear. The clothes are designed to be functional, readily identifiable and ultimately morale-sapping.

4.WORK

4 WORK

Our work uniforms are the ones we spend most time in, so we might as well enjoy them. For many of us in the West this means only one thing – the suit. We're married in it, we work in it, and then when we die we're dressed in another one and put in our coffins.

The suit evolved slowly until the 1950s, and has since – aside from the vagaries of fashion – stayed pretty much unchanged to the present day. Tailoring really took off during the thirteenth century, and during the Renaissance it started to concentrate less on hiding the human body and began instead to actively flatter and highlight the body's shape. Centres of tailoring shifted around Europe from Spain to Italy and France. But in the seventeenth century, during Louis XIV's 72-year reign, menswear took a huge leap forward and north across the English Channel to the court of Charles II. Men stopped wearing the doublet, hose and cloak and moved towards the coat, waistcoat and breeches that are the roots of the modern suit.

By the nineteenth century, men were still wearing morning suits – dark jackets with tails and non-matching pinstriped trousers. The lounge suit – with a shorter jacket in the same matching cloth as the trousers – was created as a more casual alternative for free time in the country or at the seaside. It's ironic that what we now consider as one of the most formal and restrictive outfits in our working wardrobe began life as something the Victorians and Edwardians saw as leisurewear.

Different workers had always worn uniforms to signify pride in their professional standards – the butcher wore a blue and white striped overall with a straw boater, the storekeeper and grocer might wear a beige coat – but they always wore a collar and tie underneath to distance themselves from the working classes. As the twentieth century saw a growth in commercialism, chains of shops, stores and other organizations needed to make their stamp on both their employees and the public eye. The commercial uniform in company colours was born, and with it the concept of the 'brand'.

One of the first restaurants to brand itself using uniform was the Lyons tea shop. The first one opened in London's Piccadilly in 1894, and soon there were 250 of the white and gold shops in London and its surrounding suburbs. People knew they could go into any Lyons tea shop and get a decent meal, and they knew exactly what it would cost. They also knew they would be served by waitresses known as 'nippies', who wore a distinctive uniform consisting of a black dress with two rows of buttons up the front and a large white collar, a white pinafore and a white headdress.

The nippy caught the public's imagination and children even began to dress up as nippies for local fêtes. In terms of branding, that's pretty much your job done for you! Other company uniforms of the time were inspired by the proliferation and democratization of motor-car ownership in the early part of the twentieth century. To begin with, only the very rich could afford cars, so the chauffeur took on a groom's role and his dress reflected it. He wore very much the same costume as someone who looked after horses – long, calf-length boots, jodhpurs and a smart jacket. Later, when the 'iron horse' began to reach the middle classes, groups such as the Automobile Association were set up. The AA was established in 1905 by a group of motorists who wanted to avoid police speed traps, but the organization grew a number of auxiliary arms – testing hotels, putting up danger signs on accident blackspots and offering legal advice. The AA patrolman in his smart military-style jacket (with stripes showing his rank) would salute motorists who sported the AA badge on their grille, but would conspicuously NOT salute you if there was a police speed trap ahead.

In 1950s America another brand was emerging: Playboy. The magazine's founder Hugh Hefner devised the bunny costume for his staff, to be worn at 'Playboy authorized activities'. The one-piece rayon-satin bathing suit, complete with ears and a tail, was the first service uniform ever granted a patent in the USA – number 762,884. The bunny costume moved with the times, and by the 1960s it had absorbed the psychedelic pop art popularized by fashion houses such as Pucci.

Playboy wasn't the only company trying to define itself via the uniforms of its female staff – the branding war was taking place in the air, too. In the 1960s airline stewardesses were at the front line of the battle between tightly regulated airlines as to who could stand out the most, and uniform redesigns were taking place every two years on average. Braniff's 'Braniff babes' caught the 1960s vibe with op-art tights and eye-popping pink outfits designed by Pucci, while Singapore Airlines successfully marketed itself on the strength of its doe-eyed, subservient 'Singapore girls' in traditional yet modern *sarong kebaya* uniforms designed by Pierre Balmain. By the 1970s, increased competition meant airlines had become even less subtle and Southwest Airlines unashamedly dressed its stewardesses in thigh-hugging shorts.

It's a small world, and globalization means that chains, brands and their uniforms now spread across the planet faster than ever. Your employees are your brand and it's important to get them looking right. When FedEx was looking to update its uniforms it brought in Stan Herman, the president of the Council of Fashion Designers of

Previous page A group of Singapore Airline's (SIA) flight attendants, or 'Singapore Girls'. In their distinctive sarong kebayas in batik material, designed by Pierre Balmain, they personify what SIA described as 'the tradition of friendly service and Asian hospitality'.

This page Mr Jones the butcher from the British wartime comedy television show Dad's Army in blue and white striped apron, the traditional garb of the British butcher.

America. Keeping an international workforce happy with one uniform is a challenge – US employees wanted 'wash and wear' synthetic fibres, whereas European workers wanted natural fibres. Global organizations get around problems by producing a range of separates – caps, shirts, sweaters – that can be chosen to fit different employees' tastes and needs, while simultaneously ensuring that they toe the company line.

When Ray Kroc opened the first McDonald's franchise in Des Plaines, Illinois, USA, in 1955, he probably had little idea that he'd start a fast-food revolution that would have burka-clad youths wearing McDonald's uniforms serving halal meat burgers to Muslim clientele in Paris or far-flung branches in Nicaragua and Kazakstan. Their staff may not agree, but fast-food uniforms have progressed a great deal from the days of the American 'soda jerk' who would dispense milkshakes from drugstores wearing a white military-style cap. Today over 26 million people in the USA alone wear uniforms in the fast-food business (now referred to as 'career apparel' to remove any associations with the military).

Today's young workers are choosy about their uniforms – and thus today's companies have to consider their employees' requirements to look and feel good in order to attract and retain workers. But young people are also fiercely independent and free spirited, something that puts them at odds with the whole idea of the uniform. It's a constant battle.

When someone's providing you with some sort of service, whether they're changing your tyres or serving you drinks, check out their uniform. The chances are that it will speak volumes about the organization they work for.

Parisian fast food with a distinctly non-French global influence. This picture could have been taken anywhere in the world – the uniform is the same, only the language gives the location away.

Above Commodity traders doing business in 'the pit' where a single false slip could cost millions. The 'open cry' system, with the brightly coloured identifying blazers, is increasingly being replaced by the quiet hum of electronic trading.

Opposite Three generations of Bowlers. The 'iron hat' was designed by hatters Lock & Co. of St James, London, and sent to hat-makers Thomas and William Bowler to be made. The wearing of the bowler meant different things depending on location – in London it was associated with professionals, but in the rest of the country it was associated with a higher class of servant, such as a butler or valet.

Opposite The Monty Python team delighted in ridiculing the middle classes of England in the late 1960s and early 1970s. Here John Cleese wears the uniform of the government official on his way to work with a bowler hat, suit and briefcase in the sketch 'The Ministry of Silly Walks'.

Below For the hard-working commuter the suit has also become a badge of servitude; the yoke that is worn throughout the working day.

Opposite A revue dancer at The Lido, Paris, France.

Above A female croupier in the USA wears a similar waistcoat uniform to that of her male counterparts, although her longer, thinner bow-tie with two trailing ends echoes aspects of Wild-West style.

Above right The modern bunny-girl costume has incorporated colour but is otherwise little changed from its 1960s original.

Right The Chippendales' 'uniform' of bow-tie, collar and cuffs and not much else could perhaps have been designed by ex-bunny girls who wanted to demean their subjects and get their own back on the male sex.

This American supermarket of the 1950s was at the forefront of a retail revolution replacing the counter-style 'stores'. The checkout clerks wear powder blue uniforms and name badges, and the male shoppers seem to be in a uniform too – short-sleeved white shirts.

Above Japanese department store greeters – whose job it is to bow at customers entering the premises – wearing kimonos. The kimono, meaning literally 'something worn', dates back to Japan's 400-year long Heian Period, which came to an end in 1185, and little of the kimono has changed since.

Opposite A modern supermarket checkout worker in simple shift top and short-sleeved shirt to facilitate movement.

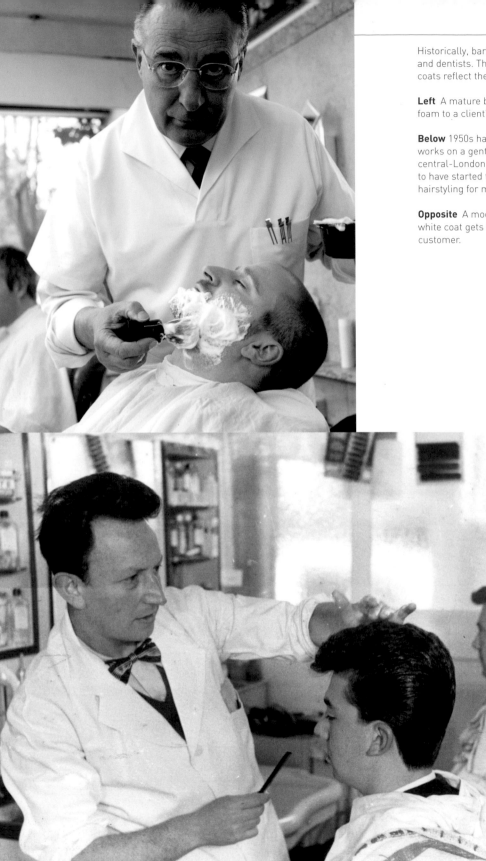

Historically, barbers were also surgeons and dentists. Their traditional white coats reflect their professional origins.

Left A mature barber applies shaving foam to a client's face.

Below 1950s hairdresser Mr Angel Rose works on a gentleman's coiffure in his central-London salon, where he claimed to have started the fashion of original hairstyling for men.

Opposite A modern barber in traditional white coat gets to grips with a ticklish customer.

This page A beautician at work. The white uniform lends her an air of calm, clean efficiency and suggests a medical element to her work. As in many other businesses, gaining a client's trust is everything.

Opposite The chemist's white coat has become a universal symbol of trust, often associated with the medical profession. It would take a large leap of faith to trust a chemist's advice if they were wearing a T-shirt.

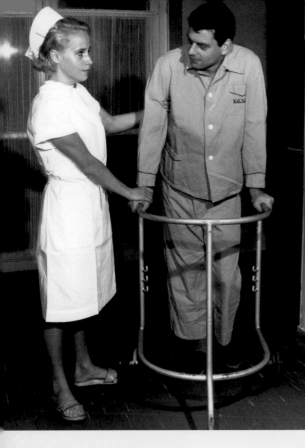

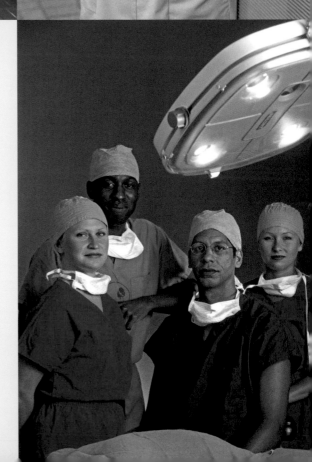

Above left and above right The nurse's uniform has been adapted from the nun's habit, because before modern hospitals, nuns cared for the ill. The modern nurse's starched pinafore emphasizes cleanliness and usually features a hat to keep stray hair in place.

Right The only time when a doctor doesn't have to wear a white coat is when he or she is operating. Here surgeons wear blue and green 'scrubs'. These were gradually introduced in the 1950s to combat eye strain caused by the effect of bright lights on white outfits, and because blood stains on white clothes are off-putting to patients.

Opposite Richard Chamberlain in the 1960s television series *Dr Kildare*. The white coat and stethoscope have always been symbols of trust, care and authority.

Above Chefs wearing the traditional white uniform and toque hat. The uniform is practical – the double-breasted jacket protects the wearer from heat and denotes cleanliness. The toque hat can be traced as far back as the sixteenth century.

Opposite A less grand but more practical modern version of the chef's toque hat performs a similar function – to prevent stray hairs from landing in food.

Opposite A Korean canteen worker serves up chicken broth with ginseng in Seoul, 2004.

This page The redoubtable British school dinner lady wearing a white apron and hat.

Opposite Waiting staff from all over the world have adopted a similar black and white colour scheme, and a tie gives an air of formality.

This page Lyons tea houses were one of the first fast-food chains in the world – 250 of the shops were doing business in the UK at their height. Their waitresses, known as 'nippies' wore white aprons and collars to indicate cleanliness and efficiency.

Above Fast food Beijing-style could involve a light snack of skewers of scorpion, grasshopper or starfish. The food may be very challenging, but the uniform, with its Nike sunshades, shows distinct globalization. Just eat it!

Opposite, top Burka-clad workers at Beurger King Moslem, Clichy-sous-Bois, Paris, France. The restaurant serves only halal meat and the burka uniforms are a sign of increasing globalization in the burgeoning world of fast food.

Opposite, bottom Another Muslim variant of fast-food uniform, this is a McDonald's restaurant in Kuala Lumpur, Malaysia.

TWA uniforms from around 1956 as modelled by five sets of stewardess twins. The pillbox hats have a distinct air-force influence.

This page This purser's uniform was developed by British Rail when designing concepts for their Advanced Passenger Train in 1974. The uniform's woollen tank top is greatly influenced by 1970s fashion of the time, and the hat shows the decade's infatuation with the space age.

Opposite In the early 1970s the airline marketing war was in full effect. America's Southwest Airlines tried to get hip with their stewardesses' uniforms. 'The girls must be able to wear kinky boots and hotpants or they don't get the job,' said the airline's (male) bosses.

Dressing to impress... the customer.

Left A dashing doorman at the Shanghai Peace Hotel hails a cab in blazer, coat and peaked cap.

Below, left This hotel doorman at the Hotel Deauville, Normandy, France, wears the classic bellhop outfit with three rows of highly polished brass buttons and a pillbox hat exhibiting a strong military influence.

Below, right A greeter at the Peace Hotel, Shanghai, in smart gold-edged uniform.

Opposite A hotel maid gives bellhops a lesson in needlework.

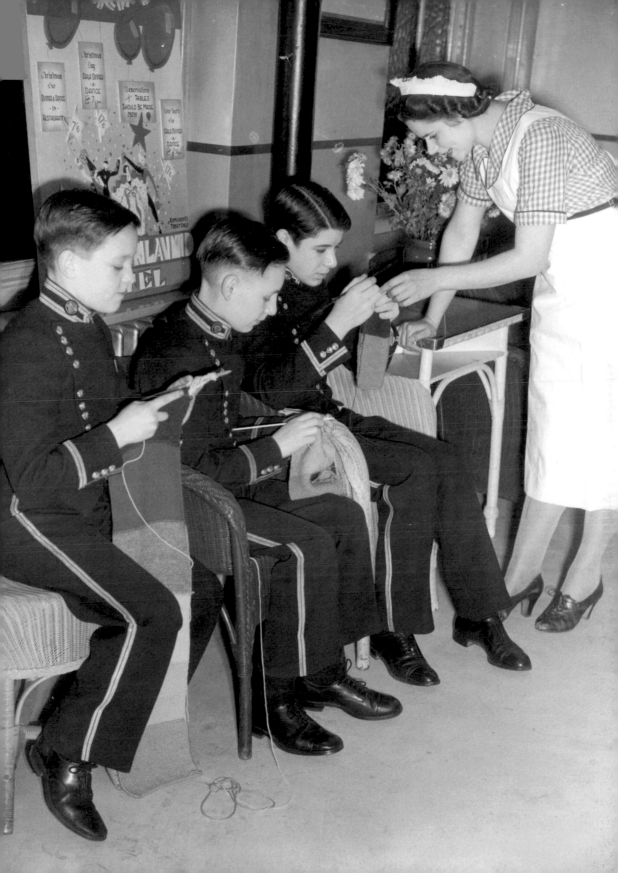

Above Cocktail hour aboard Lufthansa's
first-class 'Senator' service in 1958.
In the 1950s airlines were in their infancy
and the white-coated drinks waiter's
uniform reassures nervous flyers by
making no reference to the fact that
they are in the air or that he is part
of a flight crew.

Right The bow-tie and waistcoat of the
barman facilitates movement – a tie
might well fall into a drink – while giving
them a quiet air of smart professionalism.

Opposite, top Barmaids serving root
beer in Cleveland, Ohio, USA. The polo
shirt has now become a corporate
essential, being smarter than the T-shirt
but just about as easy to mass produce.

Opposite, bottom This white-coated
waiter keeps his eyes professionally
trained on the drinks as he serves
champagne backstage at a fashion
show in the 1950s.

Opposite, top A San Franciscan postman contemplates how hard his job would be without his Segway scooter. Red, blue and white tend to be used globally as postal uniform colours.

Opposite, bottom Ready to serve – men in bow-ties on fast-food delivery scooters in Japan.

Above left A Japanese postman, clad in a smart blue suit, speeds through the traffic on his trusty moped.

Above As with most outdoor workers, the modern postman in the UK has been given high-visibility garments as part of his uniform.

Left A UPS deliveryman enjoys a summer uniform that features matching shorts for coolness and freedom of movement.

Glowing with pride: advances in reflective fabrics have kept millions of workers safe in treacherous conditions.

Above Rescue workers from Britain's Royal National Lifeboat Institution wear orange to help show their location should they fall overboard.

Opposite, top Bright yellow identifies these Australian firefighters.

Opposite, bottom This photograph of firemen in Madrid, Spain, emphasizes the importance of the highly reflective yellow strips sewn onto their dark uniforms.

Opposite The AA (Automobile Association) patrolman wears a uniform reminiscent of equestrian garb, as befitted the new-fangled motor car's 'iron horse' status. Motoring legend has it that an AA patrolman would always salute a member – unless there was a police speed trap waiting for him around the corner!

Above The modern AA rescue patrolman in high-visibility 'DayGlo' yellow jacket. High-visibility colours such as these have greatly contributed to the safety and wellbeing of those who have to work in inclement weather and dangerous roadside situations. Shame they had to lose the riding boots, though.

5.SPORT
& LEISURE

5 SPORT & LEISURE

Barely had man learnt to walk erect before he began to develop a fascination with kicking things, notably balls. In the Middle Ages, in the so-called civilized West, football was a rough pursuit with no set teams, just whole villages kicking, punching and manhandling a pig's bladder to 'goals'. Of course, it took stylish Italians to introduce the practice of actually changing clothes for ball sports. The first rudimentary soccer strip thus appeared in sixteenth-century Florence, when young men would dress up in fine silk costumes and gather in the Piazza della Novere to play *calcio*, or 'kickball'. Alas, this too was a violent pursuit, thought to have derived from military training, and players could kick, barge or shoulder-charge their opponents. Needless to say, there were many injuries.

English public schools and universities are credited with channelling and transforming these raw, violent pursuits into 'the beautiful game' we know today. The game itself split into 'handling' games, as set out by Rugby School, and pure kicking games, as established by Cambridge and Sheffield Universities. In these fledgling days men played in whatever they turned up in, and teams were demarcated by college caps and scarves. The first proper football kits emerged in the 1870s, and their colours were usually those of the academic body or club with which their players were linked. Thus Blackburn Rovers abandoned an early garish green and white quartered strip in favour of the pale blue and white of Cambridge University, the Alma Mater of several of their founders.

English football remained a pursuit of the upper and middle classes, in part governed by uniform, since they were the only ones who could afford to buy an elaborate shirt in the club's colours. In Scotland the sport was far more democratic and working class. For the first England v. Scotland clash of 1872, the Scottish team played in the more affordable simple dark blue strip that has since become the country's sporting colour. Club colours in Scotland quickly took on religious connotations reflecting the sectarianism of the times – the Hibernian Football Club founded by Catholic Irish émigrés living in Edinburgh wore green, whereas the Protestant and Presbyterian teams favoured the colours of the Union – red, white and blue.

Sporting strips have evolved to reflect the nature of the game. Football, which allows players to pass the ball forward, developed simple strips of block colours that enable team players to stand out from a long distance. Rugby, which does not permit the forward pass, didn't need such high definition from its strips because its players were passing the ball over relatively short distances, so many remained more elaborate – quarters or hoops were (and still are) common.

American football grew out of the rugby 'handling' game, the first match being recorded in 1829 between freshman and sophomore classes at Harvard University. It was traditionally played on the first Monday of term, which was ominously dubbed 'Bloody Monday' by students because of the many injuries and deaths that occurred on the field. At its peak, 33 players were killed in just one year. The deaths and injuries had reached such an alarming rate that President Theodore Roosevelt, himself an admirer of the game, sought to ban it unless it was brought into line. Not surprisingly, one of the suggestions mooted was better protection, and this is at the root of the wide array of helmets and shoulder, elbow, knee and groin protectors seen in the NFL today.

American football is often associated with cheerleaders – enthusiastic young girls wearing team colours and wielding pompoms, who stand at the sidelines performing highly choreographed dances and chants. However, the actual practice of cheerleading was begun by a man, Johnny Campbell, who was a freshman of the University of Minnesota. In November 1898 he stood before the crowd at a football match directing the chant 'Varsity, varsity, Minn-e-Soh-TAH!' which is still used to this day. Women only took up the pompom in the 1920s.

Traditionally, cricket and tennis have both been played in white with no team demarcation. In both cases this was because it was fairly obvious which sides were which: in cricket, the men with the bats were from one side and those who weren't were the fielders. In contrast, American baseball very quickly developed team uniforms. At the turn of the twentieth century baseball shirts were predominantly white, with teams being identified by their hosiery, hence names like the Red Socks. The Washington team was the first to put their nickname on their shirts – they wore uniforms emblazoned with the word 'NATIONALS' in 1905. Gradually, colour and design crept in, like the classic baseball pinstripe that first appeared on teams' shirts in 1912. The introduction of colour television in the 1960s meant teams employed bolder and brighter strips in order to stand out, like the green and gold of the Oakland Athletics and the space-age red and yellow of the 1970s Houston Astros.

Similarly, the more restrained sports of tennis and cricket have still seen a huge sea change in their uniform style over the last century, mainly due to the introduction of colour. Tennis stars, such as the USA's 'Big' Bill Tilden and the UK's Fred Perry, turned up to play in long white trousers and woollen V-neck white jumpers in the 1920s

Previous page Keiron 'Sweet Pea' Shine (11) of the Harlem Globetrotters dribbles the ball during a show at the MCI Center, Washington DC, USA, in 2004.

This page The game of snooker has its roots in billiards, which was played by British army officers stationed in India. As such, the bow-tie and waistcoat of the player and the dinner jacket of the referee have an air of the gentleman's club about them.

and even into the 1930s – their outfits were more for decency than to facilitate movement. Women were even more restricted, wearing knee-length skirts up to World War II. Today, Wimbledon Lawn Tennis Club is alone on the international tennis circuit as still stipulating a predominantly white outfit, although it is constantly at war with tennis players and sportswear manufacturers who try to bend the rules. In 1949 Gertrude 'Gorgeous Gussie' Moran was denied her request to wear colour at Wimbledon, and so commissioned the equally colourful character, tennis player and fashion designer Ted Tinling to create a dress that displayed white lacy knickers that shocked the reactionary old guard and even became the subject of a debate in Parliament.

Even when they were at leisure, the lives of the ruling classes on both sides of the Atlantic were dominated by uniforms. The morning coat, with its cutaway front and tails, was originally worn for the morning constitutional exercise, whether on horseback or on foot, yet it has now been relegated to the echelons of high formal wear and is most commonly seen at weddings that take place in the daytime. For evening wear, the black tie and tails, or even the more formal white tie, has been replaced by the shorter tuxedo, or dinner jacket. In 1860, Edward, the dashing Prince of Wales, commissioned Savile Row tailors Henry Poole & Co. to create a more casual dinner jacket minus the tails. It was then taken up and copied by high society habitués of the famous Tuxedo Club, 40 miles northwest of New York, where it got its name.

Even today the upper classes are as obsessed by the right uniform as ever. Riding to hounds still necessitates the appropriate scarlet coat (or 'hunting pink', as it is known). Any form of country pursuit requires the wearing of tweed, the windproof, tough wool fibre that was to the eighteenth and nineteenth century what Gore-Tex and Kevlar are to today's active sportsmen. Choosing the right uniform is as much of a sport as the sport itself.

A British fox hunter in traditional 'hunting pink'. Although the coat is obviously scarlet, its pink name is said to derive from a tailor called Pink who made hunting outfits. The white stock is tied tightly around the throat and is supposed to protect the wearer's neck if he or she falls from the horse while jumping.

Above Hunters knew about camouflage well before the German Army. This gentleman wears clothes honed over years for practicality, comfort and blending in with the landscape. Tweed is a tough material and was the original hi-tech fibre: it's warm and tough, yet lets the wearer's skin breathe in active situations.

Opposite New York Yankees pitcher Roger Clemens wearing the distinctive pinstripe strip and baseball cap in 2002. The baseball pinstripe proved so distinctive it was appropriated by designer Raymond Loewy for the Lucky Strike cigarette packs.

The game of rugby is said to have been invented by one pupil, William Webb Ellis, who attended Rugby School from 1816 to 1825. This picture of the England team from the 1920s shows the game in all its gory, muddy glory.

Iron men don't need body armour, and rugby players wear little more protection than team colours.

An American football cheerleader.
Amazingly the concept of cheerleading
was begun by a man. Women entered the
fray only in the 1920s, although they did
bring in the pompom. As cheerleading
took off in the USA, the first pompoms
were painstakingly made at home from
paper. In 1953 an enterprising man
called Lawrence Herkimer founded
his Cheerleading Supply Company and
began commercially supplying pompoms.
More durable vinyl pompoms were
introduced in 1965 by Fred Gastoff.
The name comes from the French
word 'pompon'.

American football players in helmets and padded shoulder protection akin to military body armour.

Above A one-day cricket match between England and Jamaica. Modern variants of the traditional game use strips that are easily distinguishable from each other instead of the classic whites.

Opposite A classic 1980s English cricket team line-up featuring David Gower and Ian Botham. The older forms of the game – test, first-class and club cricket – are played in the traditional white uniform. Recent attempts to inject some excitement into the game have resulted in Twenty20 cricket, where teams play in coloured uniforms for differentiation.

Brazil's team colours of vivid yellow and contrasting blue stand out as Ronaldo fires a scorching free kick at the German defence in the 2002 Football World Cup. Ronaldo won the tournament with both goals in a 2-0 victory, securing Brazil's fifth World Cup win.

Above The 2007 English FA Cup Final featured Chelsea against Manchester United. Football strips are about clarity and definition, so when two teams who both wear the same coloured strip play against one another, the visiting team must wear an alternative 'away' strip.

Left In 2004 Real Madrid's star player, the Brazilian Ronaldo (left) is tackled by Real Mallorca's Guillermo Pereyra. The V-neck collarless shirt in hi-tech, moisture-wicking fabric has come a long way from the heavy cotton, long-sleeved shirts of the game's infancy.

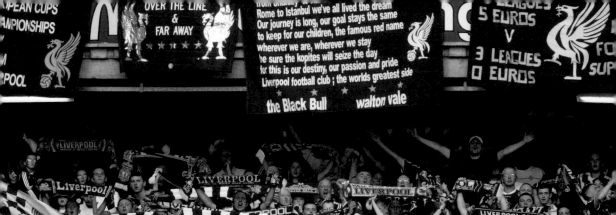

Yellow fever: Brazil fans in Paris, 2004.

Above Fencer Andrés Carrillo of Cuba in action against Rubén Limardo of Venezuela during the Gold Medal Match of the XV Pan American Games in Rio de Janeiro, 2007. The white uniforms are made of cotton and nylon with Kevlar for vulnerable areas. Fencing uniforms became much more protective after the tragic death of Soviet fencer Vladimir Smirnov in the 1982 Championships in Rome, when his opponent's blade pierced his mask, killing him nine days later.

Opposite Kendo swordsmen wear face protection and body armour. Even though the *shinai*, or sword, is made of bamboo, it can still wreak severe damage on the human body. To facilitate movement, they wear *hakama*, trousers with very wide legs. *Kendoka* fight barefoot, as in other martial arts.

Below The sport of judo is an adaptation of the Japanese martial art ju-jitsu. The standard white *judogi* uniform is tied by a belt signifying the wearer's progress from white (novice) through yellow (*gokyu*), green (*yonkyu*), brown (*sankyu*) and black (*shodan*).

Opposite The New Zealand national rugby team are known as the All Blacks, for obvious reasons, although their shirt also includes a delicate fern leaf, the unofficial symbol of New Zealand. Here they perform their ceremonial 'Haka' war dance in Hamilton, 2006.

Free fighting (where protagonists are allowed to kick as well as punch) is a mixed martial arts sport that requires little in the way of uniform, save shorts and boxing gloves, usually of one colour. Here Xing Jinxi (red shorts) of China leaps into the air to kick Fabian Silva of the USA. This free-fight competition (2006) might look anything but friendly, but it was part of an anti-terrorism cooperation initiative between the Chinese and US governments.

The ballet tutu, worn here by the Kirov Ballet (**above**) and the Moscow Academic Ballet School (**left**) was first worn by dancers of the Paris Opera in the 1800s, although at that time their thighs were hidden by large calico bloomers. The modern outfit is designed to accentuate femininity while also allowing freedom of movement.

Opposite Sumo wrestling is steeped in two millennia of Japanese tradition. Wrestlers wear a 30-ft long loincloth called a *mawashi*, which has *sagari* tucked into the front, representing the sacred ropes of Shinto shrines. The number of *sagari* is always odd, and between 17 and 21 – lucky numbers in the Shinto tradition.

Opposite, top A wrestler purifies the ring with salt before a bout.

Dancers at the Edinburgh Highland Games. Traditional Highland dress consisted of a Breacan Feile – five yds of tartan material secured around the waist and loins with a leather belt and fastened to the left shoulder with a large brooch, leaving the right arm free for swordsmanship.

Above Olympic athletes from the USA in their travelling and formal uniforms, 1948. Such off-field uniforms are meant to create a feeling of smart uniformity and team spirit even when the athletes are not performing.

Above right Great Britain's Henley Royal Regatta is a riot of colour as men of all ages squeeze into the old brightly coloured rowing club blazers they wore when they were young, lean, fit rowers.

Opposite, top The European Ryder Cup Team of 2006 pose in pink blazers that at least match their complexions.

Opposite, bottom Golf is not a sport renowned for its style. Plus-fours may have given way to polo shirts, but most clubs still insist on players wearing a shirt with a collar on the greens. Here the American Ryder Cup team wear traditional blue blazers combined with some ill-advised patterned shirts more suited to pyjamas.

Above left Rowing headgear can either mean a straw boater trimmed with a club ribbon or a cap in the club's colours. A collar and tie are prerequisites, and ladies must wear a skirt or dress down to the knee.

Above right Venus and Serena Williams have pushed the tennis strip about as far as it will go. Gone is the white that used to be a staple of the sport. Today's outfits are about performance and impact rather than ladylike modesty.

Opposite A lady plays tennis in 1914, an era when modesty still dictated women's sporting uniforms. Movement around the court was severely restricted given the long, heavy, tight-waisted skirts and long-sleeved top.

This page Men's tennis outfits weren't much less restrictive. Here a man plays in long flannel trousers and a sweater normally associated with cricket. Careful, Sir, you might catch a chill!

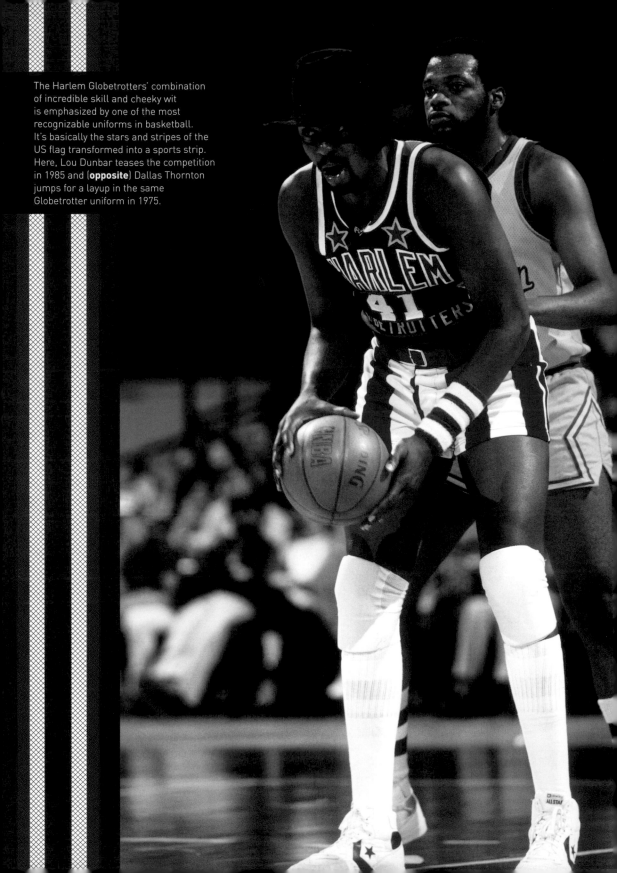

The Harlem Globetrotters' combination of incredible skill and cheeky wit is emphasized by one of the most recognizable uniforms in basketball. It's basically the stars and stripes of the US flag transformed into a sports strip. Here, Lou Dunbar teases the competition in 1985 and (**opposite**) Dallas Thornton jumps for a layup in the same Globetrotter uniform in 1975.

Leather, as worn here by this member of the Hells Angels Motorcycle Club, has been adopted by bikers primarily as protection from the cold and from the road should they fall off. However, this pragmatic clothing has turned into a uniform that says 'biker' worldwide.

6. FUTURE & FANTASY

6 FUTURE & FANTASY

When predicting the future, forecasting what we'll wear has perhaps the greatest potential for error. Philip Francis Nowlan, writing in 1928, may have set the adventures of his American hero Buck Rogers comfortably far off in the twenty-fifth century, but spare a thought for Brit Frank Hampson, the illustrator of 'Dan Dare', who, writing in the 1950s, had a confused idea of how technology would advance in the following decades. Although Dan is said to be born in 1967, he is a member of Spacefleet and wears a spacesuit based on British diving suits. When he's not in space, his uniform is similar to that worn by the British Army (unsurprisingly: Hampson used his own World War II uniform as a model). Now I don't want to nit-pick, but I was born around the same time as fictional Dan, and I want to know – where's my spacesuit?

The reason for such technological optimism was that man was on the brink of space, the 'final frontier'. By the 1960s the space race was fully underway and everything in popular culture from fashion to music was influenced by space. Cue Gene Roddenberry's 1966 television series *Star Trek*. The series was funny, often camp, but with an important message of integration and understanding between species, and that message of equality was mirrored in its *Starfleet* uniforms. Epaulettes and insignia of rank were abandoned in favour of loose fitting tops in different colours to convey a crew member's role: red for engineering and security, blue for science and medicine, and gold for command. The uniforms were made of that very 1960s fabric, velour, and shrank when dry cleaned, which explains why they look uncomfortably tight in some episodes. *Star Trek*, perhaps the most swinging space series to come out of the 1960s, used a young designer called William Ware Theiss to design some of its more outlandish and sexy costumes. He espoused what he called the 'Theiss theory of titillation' which stated that 'The degree to which a costume is considered sexy is directly proportional to how much it looks like it's about to fall off.'

By 1968, the concept of the camp, vampish space costume had reached its peak with Roger Vadim's *Barbarella*. Dressed in a melange of plastic, chain mail, Spandex and boots designed by Paco Rabanne, Vadim's then-wife Jane Fonda strides around space in an essentially male fantasy role. 'The space age adventuress, whose sex-ploits are among the most bizarre ever seen' ran the film's tagline. A more intelligent view of space and the future is provided by Stanley Kubrick's *2001: A Space Odyssey*, made in the same year, 1968. The spacesuit uniforms are brightly coloured but extremely futuristic, while the space stewardesses' uniforms are as outlandish as the real uniforms that air stewardesses were required to wear in the 1960s.

Sci-fi slumbered in the cinema for nearly a decade until George Lucas' *Star Wars* reignited the genre, hitting the box offices in 1977. Not only was the film remarkable for its vision and special effects, it also had great uniforms. The Imperial Stormtroopers wore white body armour and helmets with no visible demarcation of rank. The concept was a clever one, hiding the actors' faces and dehumanizing them into cold killing machines. It was an inspired decision to make the armour white – black would have been too obvious a shorthand for evil, and was reserved for the ultimate baddie, Darth Vader, reminiscent of the chilling female robot in Fritz Lang's *Metropolis*, made 50 years earlier in 1927.

Ridley Scott's *Alien* (1979) put a different spin on uniforms of the future – grim reality. The crew of the *Nostromo* are tired and bored of space travel. It no longer has the glamorous thrill of *Star Trek* – rather, it is a tedious slog, and their low morale is reflected in their shabby, dilapidated uniforms. You can almost smell the stale air and sweat.

So what will uniforms really be like in the future? We don't want to fall into the Dan Dare trap, but we do feel empowered to make a few predictions.

WORKWEAR

When times are good, it tends to be reflected in our workwear. The monetary boom of the 1980s was born out in the exuberance of the suits of the period – double-breasted, worn with loud, novelty ties. During times of financial insecurity, employees of both sexes will seek not to stand out but to conform. And conformity means a return to the sober suit – it's stylish, it means business and it's built to last. The only change will be in the fabric. Shortages of materials such as wool and cotton will see mankind searching for different sources of fibre. Shirts, once made of cotton, one of the most polluting fibres to produce, could be made from bamboo fibre or even rice straw. Just like cotton and flax, this is composed largely of cellulose. Better it goes into making your new work shirt than ending up as rubbish – at present rice straw accounts for 580 million t of waste every year. Likewise, chicken feathers weigh in at a shocking four billion lbs of waste per year in the USA alone. Feathers are made largely of keratin, just like wool, and can be processed into fibres to make your new work suit.

MILITARY

The stage is set for a new generation of soldier, essentially a world enforcer. The soldiers of the future will be fewer in number and perhaps less motivated in terms of national pride and will thus understandably demand better protection to do their job.

Previous page The *Thunderbirds* television series, although created in the 1960s, was set in the twenty-first century. The designers came up with this timeless yet modern outfit that appears to combine influences from the Canadian air force in its cap and a bold sash for the staff of International Rescue.

This page Space-age design was at its apogée in the 1960s, and it influenced every strata of life. Here, the 1964 James Bond film *Goldfinger* shows futuristic leanings in its choice of costume for Pussy Galore's Flying School girls – broad white belts and boots and tight black suits.

The American military reckons its Future Force Warrior initiative will be ready for combat by 2010. One of the biggest drawbacks of current combat uniforms is their heaviness – soldiers fighting in Iraq and Afghanistan often carry 120lbs of external weight. The new uniform is a mere 50lbs, yet delivers better protection. A second phase, called Future Warrior 2020, is more ambitious still. Nanotechnology could create fibres in the uniform that will twitch to simulate muscles and could give soldiers of the future almost superhuman strength; at least 25–35 per cent greater lifting capacity.

Future uniforms may also benefit from 'liquid armour'. Shear Thickening Fluid, or STF, is a combination of polyethylene glycol and microscopic glass particles that moves with the soldier's body yet hardens instantly on impact with a fast-moving external force such as a bullet or piece of shrapnel.

SPACE

Those bulky uniforms worn by astronauts in the first years of space exploration were developed from the flying overalls worn by high-altitude bomber pilots, and not much has changed in the intervening 40 years – until now. A new, NASA-sponsored project by the Massachusetts Institute of Technology may enable tomorrow's astronauts to move as freely as they do on Earth. The BioSuit will weigh a mere 40lbs, compared with today's 300-lb 'Michelin Man' space suits. The bulk in traditional space suits was needed to pressurize the astronaut's bodies against the vacuum of space (current NASA spacesuits have 14 gas-pressurized layers) but the BioSuit replaces this with a rigid skeleton encasing the body like a web. It's made of Nylon, Spandex and 'shape memory polymer' and will protect the wearer from the extremes of space – 135°C in direct sunlight and -82°C in the shade. Expect to see them in use when NASA returns to the Moon, planned for around 2018. Suddenly, the supple space uniforms from Stanley Kubrick's *2001: A Space Odyssey* have become a reality, although admittedly about 17 years late.

Hi-tech stewardesses in Stanley Kubrick's sci-fi classic *2001: A Space Odyssey*. The costumes borrow a great deal from some of the more elaborate stewardess outfits that were arising from increased competition among the airlines of the 1960s, when the film was made (1968).

Opposite An improbable and perhaps impractical view of nurses of the future, as envisioned in the 1960s.

This page Braniff Airlines' stewardesses were known as 'Braniff babes' and their 1966 uniforms reflected the style of the 'swinging sixties'. The airline commissioned Italian fashion designer Emilio Pucci to produce some eye-wateringly colourful uniforms in psychedelic colours. Even in the 1960s, those bowler hats must have felt ridiculous.

Stanley Kubrick's 1971 film of Anthony Burgess's novel *A Clockwork Orange* starred Malcolm McDowell as the leader of a group of ultra-violent teenage misfits. Their home-made uniform of white boiler suits, black bowler hats, one mascaraed eye and codpieces manages to be intimidating, futuristic and stylish. When the film came out there were several violent copycat crimes committed by youths wearing the same outfits.

Opposite Riot police in full body armour including knee pads, shin protectors and thigh armour. Combined with their body armour, helmets and riot shields, they are virtually impregnable.

Above The 1998 thriller *Starship Troopers* starred (from left) Seth Gilliam, Casper Van Dien and Jake Busey. The fantasy troopers' body armour and helmets echoes that used by many riot police of the twenty-first century.

The 1982 movie *Tron* combined real actors and video effects and was revolutionary for its day. The hero is a hacker who lands inside a virtual computer-game world. The futuristic uniform, helmet and silicon-chip graphics add to the sense of being trapped in an alien electronic world.

The original television series *Star Trek* began in 1966 and thus the Starfleet uniforms, designed by William Ware Theiss, had a very 1960s slant on how space uniforms might develop in the future. In retrospect the decision to make them tight might not have been such a wise move – but then no one knew then that the same actors would be wearing them well into the mid-1980s. The velour tunics of the first and second series apparently shrank drastically when washed, also explaining the tight look.

By 1987 the original 1960s cast had made way for *Star Trek: The Next Generation*. *Starfleet* uniforms now had more of a military influence than the originals. They had richer colours and were more flattering ... but still just as tight.

In the 1960s, the most obvious colour shorthand for 'space age' was white or silver. However, Stanley Kubrick's science-fiction film *2001: A Space Odyssey* (1968) rewrote the rules, dressing its astronauts in a spectrum of colours from yellow to deep orange or red, as seen here in Keir Dullea's futuristically shaped helmet and suit (**opposite, top**). Fact caught up with fiction when NASA started to use the colour for its astronauts' suits.

This page The crew of the ill-fated US space shuttle *Columbia*, photographed as they leave crew headquarters at Kennedy Space Centre, Florida for their short and fatal flight in 2003.

Opposite, bottom Commander Eileen Collins, the first female commander of an American space shuttle, with her crew in 1999.

Above The original seven Project Mercury astronauts wearing their space uniforms: front row, left to right, Walter Schirra, Donald Slayton, John Glenn and Malcolm Carpenter. Back row, left to right, are Alan Shepard, Virgil Grissom and Gordon Cooper.

1982's *Tron* (**above, right**) and Kubrick's *2001: A Space Odyssey* (**right**) based much of their costume on real space suits.

Opposite, top March 1969 – the crew of *Apollo 11*, the first manned spaceflight to land on the moon. The crew members are, from left to right, Neil Armstrong, Michael Collins and Edwin 'Buzz' Aldrin. The space race between the USA and Russia led to the space suit being branded as a uniform.

Opposite, bottom Space-age costumes from *The Wild Wild West Revisited*, a 1979 television thriller that blended classic Western elements with James Bond-esque espionage thriller and science-fiction concepts. In the tradition of classic cinematic Bond, it featured gorgeous women and insane plots to destroy the planet.

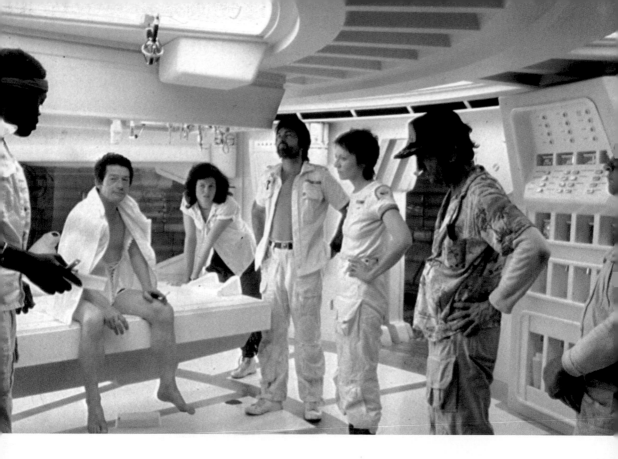

Imagine the longest, worst flight you've
been on and then extend that... for years.
Alien exploded the myth of space travel
as a glamorous career. In Ridley Scott's
1979 film the crew of the *Nostromo*
are bored, dirty and slovenly, piecing
together stale old bits of uniform
with grimy T-shirts and underwear.
Space smells.

Above In the UK television series the Cybermen are a fearsome enemy of time-travelling sci-fi hero Dr Who. On closer inspection, however, their suits have a distinctly home-made look, incorporating practice golf balls sprayed silver.

Opposite In the dystopian film *Planet of the Apes* (1968), apes were the dominant species and man the subjugated beast. The apes' costumes of leather and body armour emphasized their warlike authority.

This page Leather is still the bad boys' favourite, even in the future. The atavistic Klingons from the television series *Star Trek* borrowed some style tips from the film *Planet of the Apes*, looking formidable in leather jerkin and boots.

Opposite Roger Vadim's 1967 erotic sci-fi fantasy *Barbarella* is the most fashion oriented film ever to be set in space. Vadim hired designer Jacques Fonteray to design elaborate creations in plastic and PVC, usually incorporating thigh-high boots. The late 1960s were space-crazy, and everyone from catwalk designers to air stewardesses was wearing pseudo-futuristic styles.

This page Captain Scarlet, the indestructible hero of 'super-marionation' was said to be based on a young Cary Grant. His eponymous uniform of red jerkin, peaked cap and knee-length boots has echoes of *Star Trek* about it, and the two shows both premiered in 1967.

Opposite, top British television series *Stingray* starred Captain Troy Tempest (centre) flanked by 'Phones' Sheridan and the amphibious Marina. The male puppets' uniforms with their peaked caps, epaulettes, shiny black material and red trimming, look extremely militaristic, similar to those of the Waffen SS, an unfortunate effect that was abandoned in later 'super-marionation' films by Gerry Anderson and his team.

Opposite, bottom Here is Captain Scarlet accompanied by Captain Blue (obviously!)

The cinema has given generations of costume designers scope to explore the extremes of the uniform.

Clockwise from top left J.R.R. Tolkein's evil Orcs in Peter Jackson's 2001 *Fellowship of the Ring* wear a hotchpotch of black body armour inspired by a number of sources including Samurai, biker leather and World War II helmets.

Mike Hodges' *Flash Gordon* (1980) combines Nazi influences with elaborate helmets that derive from the future as envisaged in the original 1935 comic strip.

Mermen in the 1978 film *Warlords of Atlantis* wear sculpted body armour and sinister helmets.

The archly camp *La Decima Vittima* (*The Tenth Victim*, 1965) heralded a time in the future when people would be hunted for sport – the white costumes signify 'the future'.

Above Hitler inspecting his SS Stormtroopers with Heinrich Himmler. The helmets hark back to the old Prussian look while also being protective and – to a 1940s observer – particularly modern and intimidating.

Opposite Stormtroopers from the *Star Wars* films. The costume was designed to be protective while making the wearer appear as faceless and intimidating as possible – much like modern-day riot police. Obscure a person's eyes and you cannot reason with them. The Stormtroopers become little more than robots.

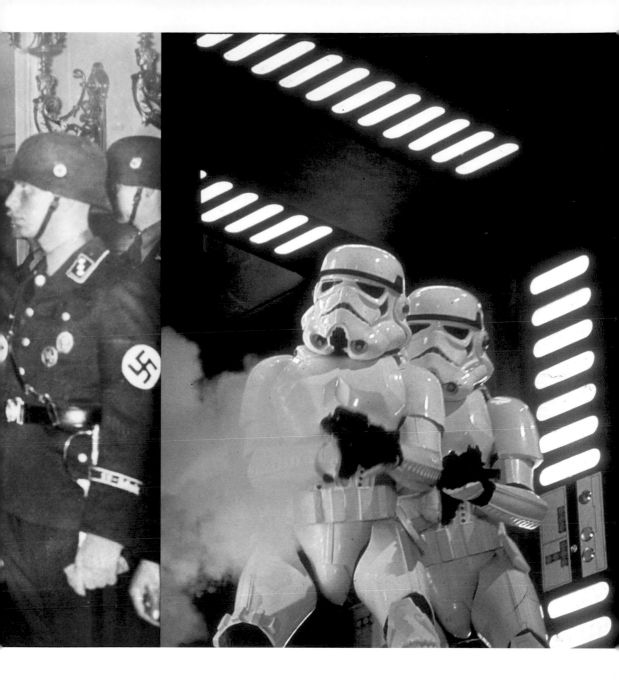

PICTURE CREDITS

Front Cover: Drum Majorette
© Corbis/Bettmann

Back Cover: Monaco policemen
© Getty Images/AFP/Valery Hache